Mysterious Encounters

Spontaneous Human Combustion

by Stuart A. Kallen

KIDHAVEN PRESS
A part of Gale, Cengage Learning

GALE
CENGAGE Learning

Detroit • New York • San Francisco • New Haven, Conn • Waterville, Maine • London

© 2009 Gale, Cengage Learning

LIBRARY OF CONGRESS CATALOGING-IN-PUBLICATION DATA

Kallen, Stuart A., 1955-
  Spontaneous human combustion / by Stuart A. Kallen.
      p. cm. -- (Mysterious encounters)
  Includes bibliographical references and index.
  ISBN 978-0-7377-4413-2 (hardcover)
  1. Combustion, Spontaneous human--Juvenile literature. I. Title.
  RA1085.K35 2009
  001.94--dc22

                                                          2008052926

KidHaven Press
27500 Drake Rd.
Farmington Hills, MI 48331

ISBN-13: 978-0-7377-4413-2
ISBN-10: 0-7377-4413-8

Printed in the United States of America
 2 3 4 5 6 7 13 12 11 10 09

Printed by Bang Printing, Brainerd, MN, 2nd Ptg., 11/2009

Contents

Chapter 1

Bursting Into Flames

Fire is a powerful force. It can reduce forests, homes, and even entire cities to smoke and ash. As frightening as fires are, most blazes can be explained. Forest fires are often traced to lightning, for example. House fires can be caused by bad wiring, furnace problems, or gas leaks.

There is one type of fire that is mysterious and unexplainable. It is called **spontaneous** human **combustion**, or SHC. *Spontaneous* means the fires start quickly, without a clear cause. *Combustion* is the process of burning. A good example of a human bursting into flames without cause or warning took place in 1966.

Irving J. Bentley was a retired Dr. living in Cloudersport, Pennsylvania. Bentley was 92-years-old and in poor health. He needed a walker, or walking frame, to keep his balance when he moved about his house. When someone knocked on the door, he was unable to get up and answer quickly. For that reason, Bentley gave a key to his front door to the gas meter reader Mr. Gosnell.

On December 5, Gosnell let himself into Bentley's house. He went to the basement to read the gas meter. Something seemed strange to him. Gosnell smelled a sickly sweet odor and saw light blue smoke hanging in the air. He went upstairs to check on Bentley. Gosnell looked in the bathroom and saw

The charred remains of Dr. Irving J. Bentley in 1966.

Very high temperatures are needed to set human tissue on fire. This is the case when people are cremated after death.

a shocking sight. On the floor lay Bentley's remains. It looked like the Dr. had been **cremated**. That is, his body had been burned until little remained but ashes. The only thing that had not burned was the lower half of Bentley's right leg. His slipper was still on the foot.

Puzzling Questions

Bentley's body had burned a hole through the floor. This let the pile of ashes that had been his body fall into the basement. Although a very hot fire is needed to burn up a human body, the rest of the house was not damaged. The nearby bath-tub was barely burned. Bentley's walker lay across the hole in the floor. The walker was only lightly touched by the fire. The rubber tips on its legs were undamaged.

Seeing the horrible sight, Gosnell ran from the house to get help. The fire department quickly arrived. Fire investigators were faced with a series of puzzling questions. How did Bentley suddenly catch fire with no visible spark or flame? How did his body burn so completely?

Human flesh is very difficult to **ignite**. It will not easily burn on its own, like a wooden log. Very high temperatures are needed to set human tissue on fire. For example, when a funeral home cremates a body it is placed in a furnace heated to 1800°F (980°C). This reduces the body to ash. This tem-

Dr. Bentley's Pipe Problems

[The] pipe-smoking physician frequently dropped ashes on his clothes—as... he had done a final time. He made his way with his walker to the bathroom in a vain attempt to extinguish the flames. The fact that he shed his robe, found smoldering in the bathtub demonstrates an external rather than internal source of ignition.

Joe Nickell and John F. Fischer, *Secrets of the Supernatural*. **Buffalo, NY: Prometheus Books, p. 154.**

perature also is hot enough to melt metal or glass.

At first, investigators thought that Bentley had set himself on fire with his pipe. But the pipe was sitting next to his bed. The answer seemed to be that the Dr. had died from spontaneous human combustion. He appeared to be one of a thousand or so similar cases noted since the 1700s.

Fire from Heaven

The exact causes of spontaneous human combustion are unknown. Some think this rare event is caused by a chemical reaction within a victim's body. There are no obvious sources of **ignition** from external, or outside, heat sources. Because of the mysterious nature of SHC, it was long described by investigators as "Fire from Heaven."[1]

In 1673 Danish biologist Thomas Bartholin published the first written account of spontaneous human combustion. Bartholin wrote about a woman in Paris who burst into flames. She "went up in ashes and smoke"[2] in her bed while sleeping on a straw mattress that was not damaged by the fire.

Many cases of spontaneous human combustion reported in Europe during the century following Bartholin's book. One case was from Rheims, France, in 1725, about Nicole Millet. Millet was found burned to death in an unburned chair. All that was left was a part of her head, lower portions of her body, and a few vertebrae (bones of the spine).

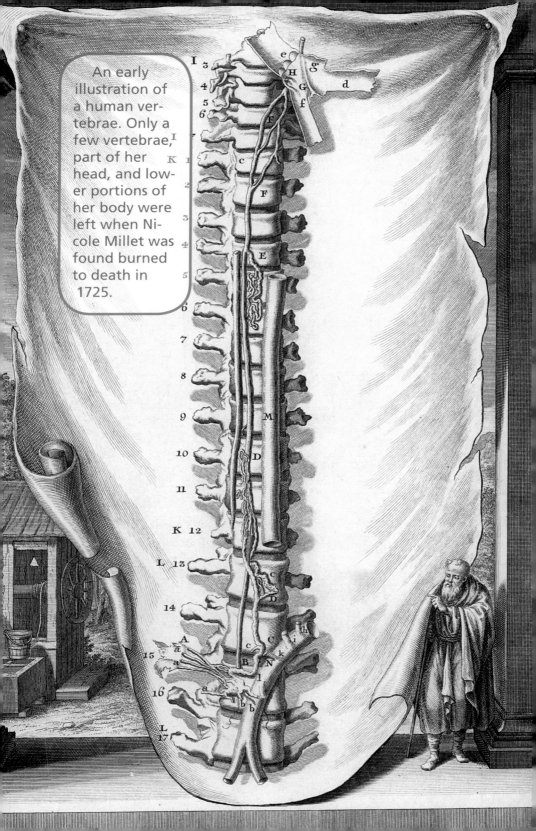

An early illustration of a human vertebrae. Only a few vertebrae, part of her head, and lower portions of her body were left when Nicole Millet was found burned to death in 1725.

Police arrested Millet's husband, Monsieur le Patron, and accused him of murder. During his trial, Patron's lawyer called in a young surgeon named Claude-Nicholas Le Cât to convince the court that Millet died from spontaneous human combustion. The defense worked. The final verdict in the case was that Nicole Millet had died "by a visitation of God."[3]

The Millet case prompted French investigator Jonas Dupont to collect facts from police investigations about all known cases of SHC. Dupont published the tales in a 1763 book called *De Incendiis Corporis Humani Spontaneis.*

An Unusual Stink

One account in Dupont's book concerns Cornelia Bandi, a 62-year-old Italian countess. Bandi went to bed, said her prayers, and fell asleep. In the morning, Bandi's maid went to wake her but the countess did not answer her knocks. The maid went outside to peer into the countess's bedroom window and saw an awful scene. Bandi's body had become a heap of ashes, but her arms and her legs remained unburned. She was still wearing stockings. Bandi's half-burned head lay between her limbs. According to investigator Giuseppe Bianchini, writing in 1731, when the heap of ashes was touched, they "left in the hand a greasy and stinking moisture. Soot floated in the air of the room and from the lower part of the window, trickled down a greasy, loathsome, yellowish liquor with an unusual stink."[4]

The description of the countess's room has been repeated in almost every case blamed on spontaneous human combustion. The body is burned, the limbs remain unharmed, and an unusual smell is noticed. The room shows no other signs of fire except for a greasy residue on walls or furniture.

However, there may be another cause for the fire that consumed Bandi. For example, the countess often rubbed her body with a strong-smelling compound called camphor. This substance was made from a type of pine sap. It produces a cool menthol feeling that relieves aches and rashes. Camphor also is extremely flammable, or able to catch fire quickly. It is possible that Bandi tripped and fell on a nearby oil lamp and set herself on fire.

An External Source?

Whatever killed the countess, it is doubtful that cases like hers from the eighteenth century will ever be solved. Bandi's is only one among many types of spontaneous combustion. Others have reported developing strange burns on their bodies with no obvious source. Some people even produce smoke from their bodies without the presence of fire. In a small percentage of cases, victims of spontaneous human combustion have survived.

Despite the mysterious circumstances surrounding SHC, there are many **skeptics**. British Dr. Gavin Thurston writes, "I can state without [a doubt] that no such phenomenon as Spontaneous Human Combustion exists or has ever occurred… the combustion is not spontaneous, it has always been started by an external source."[5]

While that may be true, police and medical investigators throughout history have been puzzled by hundreds of cases in which people burn up without warning. It remains unknown whether they were killed by fires from heaven, visitations from God, or from drunken accidents. But it matters little to the victims who were alive one minute and reduced to ashes the next.

Chapter 2

Up in Smoke

Spontaneous human combustion can strike nearly every type of person. It has killed young and old people and has taken the lives of both males and females. But some people are more likely to burst into flames. Spontaneous human combustion strikes women more often than men. Most victims are elderly and many are overweight. A large number of the dead are alone when they burn. Like most rules though, there are exceptions. There have been a few cases of teenage girls bursting into flames and even a single case of a year-old infant. The only groups that have managed to escape incidents of SHC are young boys and teenage males.

The Combustible Corpse

Perhaps the strangest case of spontaneous human combustion took place in England in 1866. A 30-year-old man who had died of typhoid was discovered burning thirteen months after his death. The remains of the unnamed man were **interred** in a church vault (tomb). According to a report of incident, the day before the fire started, "a foul smell was perceived in the church, and it was found to issue from a crevice in the floor immediately over the

This cartoon from 1853 shows a family in shock after Pa becomes a victim of spontaneous combustion after a night of drinking.

ALARMING CASE OF SPONTANEOUS COMBUSTION.

RUMMINS

BOTTLE DEPART

OLD TOM

"OH! LAW! THERE'S PA'S BOOTS—BUT WHERE'S PA?"

vault in which the coffin had been placed."[6]

The coffin had burst open and an odd liquid was oozing from within it. Church officials filled the coffin with sawdust to absorb the liquid. The next day it was discovered burning with a blue flame and "a most offensive smell."[7] None of the woodwork surrounding the coffin had burned and the church was undamaged.

The incident was blamed on spontaneous human combustion. SHC had never before been reported in a corpse. In later years, investigators guessed the incident was caused by a smoking workman. They suggest the worker threw a match onto the coffin and gases given off by the dead body started the fire. This is just a theory, however. The cause of the combustible corpse remains a mystery.

Drunken Infernos

Flaming remains are extremely rare. Among the living, people who regularly drink too much alcohol seem unusually prone to go up in smoke. Many early reports of SHC were reported among heavy drinkers.

In 1744 Grace Pett of Ipswich, England, burst into flames after drinking "a large quantity of spirituous liquor."[8] The trunk of her body was reduced to a heap of coals covered with white ash. Five years later in France, Madam De Boiseon burned up after "drinking nothing but spirits for several years."[9] Her body burned as if it had been "dipped in brandy,"[10]

Many early reports of spontaneous human combustion were reported among heavy drinkers and chronic alcoholics.

and only one leg and two hands were left after the **inferno**. In 1774 Mary Clewes of Coventry, England, who was "much addicted to drinking"[11] was found burned to death. Only one of her thighs, her spine, and her skull were left unharmed.

Skeptics say that most cases of drunken combustion can be easily solved. People who drink large amounts of liquor may set themselves on fire in many ways. This was especially true in the eighteenth and nineteenth centuries. People then relied on candles and oil lamps for light, and coal furnaces for heat. These items can be deadly in the hands of heavy drinkers. Even in modern times, thousands of drunken people die every year after passing out with lit cigarettes, cigars, and pipes. But those who believe in spontaneous human combustion point out that fires caused this way usually burn up a whole room or even an entire building. In cases of SHC, only the victim and his immediate surroundings are burned.

Burned in a Ball Dress

The most mysterious episodes of SHC do not involve heavy drinkers, cigarettes, or any other known cause. These are classic cases where combustion seems truly spontaneous. The fires burn so hot and

A Long Dress and a Lit Match

Skeptic Jan Willem Nienhuy explains how Phyllis Newcombe might have been killed when her long dress caught fire. He suggests it might not have been a cigarette that caused the fire. It could have been a match dropped by a smoker after lighting his or her cigarette.

Jan Willem Nienhuy, "Requiem for Phyllis," The Skeptical Inquirer, www.skepsis.nl/newcombe.html, March/April 2001.

so fast that little can be done to save the victims. This was the fate of Phyllis Newcombe, a 22-year-old woman from Chelmsford, England.

Unlike most cases of SHC, Newcombe was not alone when her combustion happened. In fact, she was waltzing around the crowded dance floor of Chelmsford Shire Hall with her fiancé on August 27, 1938. As the clock struck midnight, a bluish flame enveloped Newcombe as she twirled. Her fiancé tried to beat out the flames with his bare hands, but Newcombe was reduced to a pile of blackened ashes within two minutes. Writer Frank Eric Russell described the incident in 1957 and stated that Newcombe "roared like a blow-torch and no man could save her."[12]

About three weeks after the incident, a headline in the London *Daily Telegraph* newspaper told the story: GIRL BURNED IN BALL DRESS. The article quoted **coroner** L.F. Beccles: "From all my experience I have never come [across] a case so very mysterious as this."[13]

Newcombe was wearing an old-fashioned crinoline ball gown. Crinoline is a kind of netting material that gives dresses a bell shape. This dress also had wire hoops underneath to expand the skirt. Investigators blamed the fire on the dress. They assumed someone had accidentally touched a cigarette to the gown and it flamed up quickly. However, Newcombe's father took a piece of the dress material to Beccles. The men attempted to set it on fire with a cigarette but failed. The cloth did burn when a lighter was held to it. But no witnesses saw an open flame or a lit cigarette touch Newcombe's dress that night.

Black Magic and the Cinder Woman

A more typical case of spontaneous human combustion occurred in St. Petersburg, Florida, on July 1, 1951. Mary Reeser was an elderly, overweight widow who lived alone. She fit the more common profile of a SHC victim. But her awful death was different than others whose lives went up in smoke.

Reeser fell asleep in an easy chair in her apartment. Her landlady, Pansy Carpenter, checked on her at about 9:00 p.m. and did not notice anything unusual. Carpenter was awakened around 5 a.m. by the smell of **acrid** smoke. She ignored the smell

Workers clean-up the remains of Mary Reeser in her St. Petersburg, Florida, apartment in 1951.

A Simpler Explanation

The official FBI report on Mary Reeser's death gave this simple explanation:

Mrs. Reeser habitually took two sleeping pills before retiring. There is every possibility, while seated in the overstuffed chair, she became drowsy or fell asleep while smoking a cigarette, thus igniting her... housecoat. The nightgown, being highly flammable, could have... burst into flame, causing almost immediate death.

Quoted in Michael Harrison, *Fire From Heaven*. New York: Methuen, 1977, p. 130.

and went back to sleep. She went to check on Reeser again at 8 a.m. The door to Reeser's apartment was burning hot. Carpenter screamed after touching the doorknob, and two nearby workmen came running. They pushed open the door and were greeted by a blast of hot air. But they could see nothing wrong except a small piece of wood around a doorway that burned with a low flame. Since they could not find Reeser, Carpenter and the workmen assumed the elderly woman had left her apartment.

The fire department was called. When they

arrived, they put out the small fire with an extinguisher. When they inspected the apartment, they discovered a charred area in the middle of the floor, about 4 feet (1.2m) in diameter. Inside the circle, blackened chair springs were mixed with ashes. Reeser's 175-pound (79k) body, and the armchair had been reduced to 10 pounds (4.5k) of remains. These included a piece of spine, one foot wearing a black satin slipper, a small pile of ashes, and a shrunken skull the size of a teacup. The walls were coated with an oily, stinky soot.

Although her body burned at an extremely high temperature, Reeser's furniture, rugs, drapes, ceiling, and floor were barely damaged. Puzzled in-

Mystery surrounds the death of this widow, who some speculate died of spontaneous human combustion in 1958, not just a regular home fire.

vestigators could find no source for the fire. When the press learned of Reeser's manner of death, they labeled her the Cinder Woman.

Hoping to find an answer to Reeser's death, investigators brought in Dr. Wilton M. Krogman, a professor at the University of Pennsylvania's School of Medicine. Krogman was an expert on the effects of fire on the human body and helped solve unusual cases for the Federal Bureau of Investigation (FBI). Krogman estimated that Reese's body burned at a temperature of 3000°F (1649°C). But he was baffled as to the cause:

> I regard [Reeser's case] as the most amazing thing I have ever seen. As I review it, the short hairs on my neck bristle with vague fear. Were I living in the Middle Ages, I'd mutter something about Black Magic.[14]

Whatever the cause, Mary Reeser has gone down in history. No one has ever burned as completely as the Cinder Woman. She holds the title as the most totally destroyed human who ever burst into spontaneous flames.

Chapter 3

Static Electricity, Ball Lightning, and UFOs

Spontaneous human combustion is often blamed on lit cigarettes, candles, or coal furnaces. These heat sources may play a role in some SHC deaths. But on rare occasions deadly fires may be started by static electricity.

Most people have experienced the effects of static electricity after dragging their feet along a carpet or quickly pulling on a wool sweater. This creates a small electrical charge that produces a mild shock.

Static also causes sparks that may be seen in a dark room. This form of static electricity is surprising but harmless. However, when static electricity builds up in clouds it produces deadly lightning. This powerful force of nature can travel at speeds of 60,000 miles (96,560k) per second and reach temperatures of 30,000°F (16,490°C).

Ball Lightning

About forty Americans die every year after being hit by lightning. Spontaneous human combustion is not often blamed on thunderbolts, but it has been traced to a rare occurrence called ball lightning. This term refers to high voltage electrical charges that create bright light. Ball lightning appears in round shapes from the size of a pea to **spheres** 3 feet (1m) across.

The causes of ball lightning are unknown. It may be created during a lightning storm, but ball lightning behaves differently from typical lightning bolts. For example, lighting flashes last less than a fraction of a second. But ball lightning can last up to **60** seconds. Science writer Gordon Stein states that a ball of lightning that lasts one minute or more "requires an energy content so high that there is no known way for it to be formed."[15]

A Fist of Fire

The unusual properties of ball lightning have long fascinated many scientists, including G.W. Richman. In 1754 Richman was working with an assistant to measure the effects of lightning when his curiosity led to his death. Standing outdoors in a thunderstorm, a blue fireball the size of a fist emerged in the air. The ball exploded in Richman's face and caused him to catch on fire. Like victims of SHC, little of the surrounding area was damaged, but Richman was reduced to ashes in a matter of minutes.

A report of ball lightning in a less deadly form was reported in South Philadelphia in 1960. Louise

Spontaneous human combustion has been traced to a rare occurrence called ball lightning, which appears in round shapes and can generate a flash for up to sixty seconds.

Matthews was lying on a sofa when she saw a large red, flaming object enter her living room through a closed window. The mysterious fireball left the glass undamaged and did not even disturb the blinds hanging over the window. Matthews thought that an atomic bomb had been dropped on her city and hid her face in a pillow. But it was not an atomic bomb. Matthews was observing ball lightning. It passed over her and she heard a sizzling sound as all the hair burned off her head. The fireball then flew across the room and exited through another closed window.

The Blue Light of Death

The Philly fireball was a dramatic visible example of natural static electricity. But even invisible static can cause great damage. This is something the wife of an unnamed victim in Hungary understands all too well.

In May 1989, a 27-year-old engineer stopped his car near a field outside Budapest. The man got out to take in the night air. He walked about 39 feet (10m) from his car. His wife, who had stayed behind in the car, saw the man lit up by a bright blue light. He spread his arms wide and fell to the ground. The wife ran to her husband and saw that one of his tennis shoes had been blown off. Unable to help him, she flagged down a passing bus. By chance, the bus was filled with Dr.s coming from a medical conference. They examined the man and pronounced him dead.

Because of the unusual nature of the death, a coroner was contacted. He performed an **autopsy**, a medical examination conducted to determine the cause of death. The coroner found a small hole in the man's heel where his shoe had been blasted off. The lungs were damaged and his stomach and other organs were charred like burnt wood.

The man's death remains a mystery. Dr. G. Egely of the Central Institute of Physics in Budapest believes that it was spontaneous combustion caused by ball lightning:

> [The] blue light is proof of... electricity.... although the sky was cloudy [and] there were no thunderstorms in the immediate area. The body was not mostly consumed as in classical cases of human combustion, nor was a fireball observed. Still, this incident strengthens the suggestion that [invisible] ball lightning may [have prompted] spontaneous human combustion.[16]

UFO Encounters

Scientists have many questions about ball lightning and few answers. Some, like Egely, believe it can cause SHC. Others doubt that ball lightning even exists. But physical chemist David J. Turner offers a third possibility. He thinks that some reports of ball lightning may have really been unidentified flying objects, or UFOs. This would explain the appearance of fiery balls when there is no thunder or lightning. And space ships are said to hover in the air for long periods of time, behaving like ball lightning. As Turner explains, UFOs "have been reported to interact with people in strange and unpleasant ways. Several... reports document facial burning... following UFO encounters."[17]

Examples of this type of burning were widely reported in 1973 when there was an increase in UFO sightings in the western United States. Witnesses received unusual red marks on their necks just below the ear. But they could not remember how

What is thought to be a UFO is photographed flying in the sky during sunrise. Some people believe there is a connection between UFOs and spontaneous human combustion.

the marks got there. They only remember strange lights approaching them from out of the sky. They blacked out for several hours and awoke with the burns. Although none were burned beyond recognition, believers have not ruled out the connection between UFOs, ball lightning, and spontaneous human combustion.

Turner says there might even be a connection between ball lightning and ill-behaved ghosts called poltergeists. There have been thousands of reports of poltergeists destroying furniture, shrieking, throwing rocks, and causing smelly substances to drip from walls. Fire also is associated with these reckless ghosts. They have been blamed for setting bedding, chairs, and clothing on fire, sometimes killing their victims.

While such cases are extremely rare, they continue to baffle scientists, coroners, and chemists. But the source of the fire matters little to burn victims. Against the odds, these people are injured or killed by random balls of fire with no known source or explanation.

Chapter 4

Wicks, Fats, and Fires

Most cases of spontaneous human combustion are carefully investigated by police, fire officials, and coroners. Many times investigators discover other causes for the death. Sometimes the victims were murdered by being doused in gasoline and set on fire. Other times, smoking, nearby flames, portable heaters, or faulty electrical wiring are to blame. But police reports show that some cases cannot be explained. The only answer seems to be spontaneous human combustion.

Compared with the hundreds of burning deaths reported every year the number of SHC cases is small. There are maybe one or two a year in the

Oily Rags

There are real reports of spontaneous combustion in nonhuman objects. For example, many house fires have been caused by oily rags carelessly left together in a pail. Oxygen can raise the temperature in the middle of the rag pile until the flammable oil spontaneously combusts.

United States. But the small number deaths does not mean their cause is unimportant. Friends and relatives of victims seek answers. As a result, scientists continue to study the mysteries of spontaneous human combustion.

Flammable Gases

Two things are needed for the human body to explode into flames. There needs to be a flammable substance to start the fire and it needs to burn at an intense heat. These conditions are met when a body is cremated. Natural gas provides the substance that burns at a high heat. But when people burn up from SHC in their homes, there is no such flammable substance. This has led researchers to develop several theories.

One explanation for spontaneous human combustion relates to **biology**, or the physical makeup of humans. After people eat, they digest food in their stomachs. This process nourishes the body and also produces waste products. These include flammable gases made of nitrogen and hydrogen. The gases usually exit the body through flatulence (farting). However, some people believe that SHC is a result of these gases building up in the intestines. The gases are somehow ignited by enzymes or proteins, substances that the body naturally produces to aid physical functions.

However, skeptics point out several flaws with this theory. Most victims of SHC are burned on the outside. Their internal organs are often the only things left after the blaze. Therefore, the fire could not have started internally. In addition, all animals produce the flammable gas methane as a waste product when they digest food. As cattle farmer Kevin Daley points out, cows produce great quantities of methane:

> [Over] the thousands of years that Mankind has kept cattle we have… not [seen] a single… instance of the Dreaded Exploding Cow. Given the close association between cattle and methane, it could reasonably be expected that if even one were to spontaneously erupt into flames it could have serious consequences for the whole herd and any bystanders.[18]

Burning a Pig

Cows may not provide answers to the causes of spontaneous human combustion. But pigs have, according to Dr. John De Haan of the California Criminalistics Institute. In 2000 De Haan ran tests on a dead pig to learn about SHC. He wrapped an entire pig carcass in a cotton blanket. Then he soaked it in gasoline and set it on fire with a cigarette. As the pig burned, its body fat soaked into the cotton. This kept the carcass burning for hours at a very high temperature that reached 1800°F (980°C). De Haan explained how his experiment

Experiments where dead pigs are lit on fire have generated results that may explain how spontaneous human combustion occurs in people.

was similar to many SHC deaths that involve over-weight people wrapped in blankets or wearing cotton robes and smoking cigarettes:

> The elderly, the [sick], and sometimes the inebriated [drunk] are the ones that are most likely to start an accidental fire in their bedding or clothes.... So the fire starts… near them, but not on them, and then it's the fire from the [cotton clothes and] furnishing that actually gets the process going.[19]

The Wick Effect

When the fat of a burning pig soaks into cotton cloth, it creates something called the wick effect. This is similar to what happens when a candle burns. A candle is made of a cotton wick surrounded by wax. The wax is made from a flammable substance such as tallow (beef fat) or paraffin, a petroleum-based product. When a candle is lit, the burning wick soaks up the melted wax that surrounds it. This allows a candle to burn for hours without destroying the wick. When the wax is consumed, the candle burns out.

In cases of spontaneous human combustion the victim is like an inside-out candle. The flammable body fat is on the inside while the wick-like clothing or blankets are on the outside. When a heat source, such as an oil lamp, candle, or cigarette, are added, the wicking starts on fire. As it burns, it

In cases of spontaneous human combustion, the victim is like an inside-out candle, with the flammable body fat on the inside while the wick-like clothing or blankets are on the outside.

draws the fat out of the skin. This allows the victim to burn slowly at a very high temperature. Scientists believe that this is why people can be completely consumed from SHC while nearby items are not destroyed.

The wick effect also answers why a victim's legs are not usually consumed by flames. Fire burns up, not down. And the hottest part of a flame is just above the tip, not the bottom. Therefore, if a person drops a lit cigarette in his or her lap, the flames will burn up. The fire will consume the body and head while leaving the lower limbs intact. In addition, the legs are not often covered with cloth, the wick that aids in burning.

More Fat, More Fuel

The wick effect might explain why certain types of

people tend to be affected by SHC. In eight out of ten cases, the victims are female. And whatever the gender, a large percentage are overweight or alcoholics. Researcher Guy Coates explains why this matters:

> Women and overweight people have a greater amount of... fat [under the skin]. (Alcoholics also tend to be overweight). The excess fat is usually found on the torso [upper body] and thighs. The more fat that is present then the more fuel is available for the body to burn independently. The areas that are usually the most badly damaged in cases of SHC are exactly those areas that have the largest concentration of fatty tissues (the torso and thighs).[20]

Dangers of Alcohol

A European study showed that about half of all people who die alone in fires in closed rooms have high levels of alcohol in their blood. Such cases are sometimes blamed on spontaneous human combustion. But facts show that the victims fell asleep while smoking.

The ashes of an old woman—who died in 1963, allegedly the result of spontaneous human combustion—are scattered throughout her room.

The flaming fat would also produce the oily, smelly smoke and weird yellow liquid found at SHC sites.

To date, the wick effect seems to be the best explanation for the spontaneous human combustion mystery. But the theory does not apply to the small percentage of SHC victims who are thin, not drinking alcohol, and not exposed to a heat source. In these cases a human body burns without warning. This has been blamed on static electricity, UFOs, or a fire from heaven. Whatever the answer, it must be a lonely and frightening way to die.

Notes

Chapter 1: Bursting Into Flames

1. Quoted in Michael Harrison, *Fire From Heaven.* New York: Methuen, 1977, p. 2.
2. Quoted in Meredith Yayanos, "SHC: It Happens Sometimes. People Just Explode," Coilhouse, http://coilhouse.net/2008/01/03/shc-it-happens-sometimes-people-just-explode, January 3, 2008.
3. Quoted in Garth Haslam "Nicole Millet's Fiery Death," Anomalies, http://anomalyinfo.com/articles/sa00016.php, 2008.
4. Quoted in Joe Nickell and John F. Fischer, *Secrets of the Supernatural.* Buffalo, NY: Prometheus Books, 1988, pp. 161-162.
5. Quoted in Harrison, *Fire From Heaven*, p. 3.

Chapter 2: Up in Smoke

6. Quoted in Alfred Swaine Taylor, *The Principles and Practice of Medical Jurisprudence.* London: J. & A. Churchill, 1934, p. 706.
7. Quoted in Taylor, *The Principles and Practice of Medical Jurisprudence*, p. 706.
8. Quoted in Nickell and Fischer, *Secrets of the*

Supernatural, p. 163.

9. Thomas Trotter, *An Essay, Medical, Philosophical, and Chemical, on Drunkenness*. New York: Arno Press, 1981, p. 84.

10. Quoted in Nickell and Fischer, *Secrets of the Supernatural*, p. 163.

11. Quoted in Harrison, *Fire From Heaven*, p. 17.

12. Quoted in Jan Willem Nienhuy, "Requiem for Phyllis," *The Skeptical Inquirer*, vol. 25, no. 2 (March/April 2001), www.skepsis.nl/newcombe.html

13. Quoted in Nienhuy, "Requiem for Phyllis," *The Skeptical Inquirer*.

14. Quoted in E. Randall Floyd, *Great Southern Mysteries*. New York: Barnes & Nobel Publishing, 2000, p. 80.

Chapter 3: Static Electricity, Ball Lightning, and UFOs

15. Quoted in "Strange & Unexplained - Ball Lightning," Skygaze.com, www.skygaze.com/content/strange/BallLightning.shtml, 2008.

16. Quoted in "Spontaneous Human Combustion and Ball Lightning?" Science Frontiers Online, no. 17 (January-February 1991), www.science-frontiers.com/sf073/sf073b06.htm.

17. David J. Turner, "The Missing Science of Ball Lightning," *Journal of Scientific Exploration*, vol. 17, no. 3, www.scientificexploration.org/jse/articles/pdf/17.3_turner.pdf, 2003.

18. Quoted in Todd Venezia, "FBI Debunks Spontaneous Human Combustion," Rense.com, www.rense.com/general3/debunks.htm, August 4, 2000.

19. Quoted in Venezia, "FBI Debunks Spontaneous Human Combustion," Rense.com, www.rense.com/general3/debunks.htm, August 4, 2000.

20. Guy Coates, "Spontaneous Human Combustion," The AFU & Urban Legends Archive, http://tafkac.org/death/spontaneous.human. combustion/spontaneous_human_combustion.html, December 14, 1993.

Glossary

acrid: A smell or taste that is unpleasantly strong or bitter.

autopsy: The medical examination of a dead body carried out to determine the causes and conditions of death.

biology: The physical makeup and functions of plant and animal life.

combustion: A process in which something burns.

coroner: A public official responsible for investigating suspicious deaths.

cremate: To burn a dead body until it is reduced to nothing but ashes.

ignite: To catch fire.

ignition: The process of setting something on fire.

inferno: A very intense fire.

interred: Buried in a grave or placed in a tomb.

skeptic: A person who questions commonly accepted beliefs.

sphere: Any ball-shaped object.

spontaneous: Beginning suddenly without clear cause or warning.

For Further Exploration

Books

Sylvia Browne, *Secrets & Mysteries of the World*. Carlsbad, CA: Hay House, 2005. This book covers mysterious places, strange creatures, and unexplained mysteries such as spontaneous human combustion and UFOs.

E. Randall Floyd, *Great Southern Mysteries*. New York: Barnes & Nobel Publishing, 2000. A book full of scary and mysterious stories from the southern United States including the tales human torches and fires from heaven.

Judith Herbst, *Beyond the Grave*. Minneapolis, MN: Lerner Publications, 2005. Examines and explains several mysteries surrounding death and dying, including spontaneous human combustion.

Internet Sources

Garth Haslam, "Spontaneous Human Combustion," Anomalies, www.anomalyinfo.com, 2008. Dozens of stories about SHC with links to pages about the legend, history, types of SHC, explanations, and a timeline.

Joe Nickell, "Investigative Files: Fiery Tales That

Spontaneously Destruct," Committee for Skeptical Inquiry, www.csicop.org/si/9803/shc.html, 2006. A skeptic discusses the myths surrounding SHC and provides links to other articles on spontaneous human combustion.

"Spontaneous Human Combustion," Castle of Spirits, www.castleofspirits.com/shc.html, 2003. An examination of the case Mary Reeser and other, more recent, victims of SHC.

"Strange & Unexplained - Ball Lightning," Skygaze.com, www.skygaze.com/content/strange/BallLightning.shtml, 2008. An article about the odd phenomenon known as ball lightning with links to other unexplained mysteries such as the Bermuda Triangle.

Index

Picture Credits

About the Author

Stuart A. Kallen has written more than 250 books for children and young adults on topics ranging from astronomy to zoology. When not working on his next book, he can be found singing and playing guitar, or riding his bike along the beach in San Diego, California.